Crypto Investing for Beginners

PRESENTED TO

FROM

DATE

Volume · edition: __ Year: ___

This Book Belongs To

if found, please return to its owner — thank you

◇

This book belongs to: ______________________________

Phone: ____________________ **Email:** ____________________

HOME · RETURN ADDRESS

IF FOUND, PLEASE CONTACT

REWARD IF RETURNED ✓

NOTES · IMPORTANT DETAILS

In use from: ____________________ **To:** ______________

Crypto Log

on-chain · DCA · the long-term thesis

Wallet · cold / hot: ______ Today · trade #: _____

TRADES

Date	Coin	Side	Entry	Exit	Qty	PnL

COLD STORAGE · SEED BACKED UP?

HOT WALLET · GAS FEES THIS WEEK

THESIS · WHY THIS COIN

DCA SCHEDULE · WEEKLY AMOUNT

SECURITY HYGIENE

- ☐ Seed offline
- ☐ 2FA on
- ☐ Hardware wallet
- ☐ Multi-sig
- ☐ Tested recovery
- ☐ No screenshots

MACRO · ON-CHAIN METRICS · THE CYCLE STAGE

Next thesis check · unlock event:

Crypto Log

on-chain · DCA · the long-term thesis

Wallet · cold / hot: ______ Today · trade #: ______

TRADES

Date	Coin	Side	Entry	Exit	Qty	PnL

COLD STORAGE · SEED BACKED UP?

HOT WALLET · GAS FEES THIS WEEK

THESIS · WHY THIS COIN

DCA SCHEDULE · WEEKLY AMOUNT

SECURITY HYGIENE

- ☐ Seed offline
- ☐ 2FA on
- ☐ Hardware wallet
- ☐ Multi-sig
- ☐ Tested recovery
- ☐ No screenshots

MACRO · ON-CHAIN METRICS · THE CYCLE STAGE

Next thesis check · unlock event:

Crypto Log

on-chain · DCA · the long-term thesis

Wallet · cold / hot: ______ Today · trade #: ______

TRADES

Date	Coin	Side	Entry	Exit	Qty	PnL

COLD STORAGE · SEED BACKED UP?

HOT WALLET · GAS FEES THIS WEEK

THESIS · WHY THIS COIN

DCA SCHEDULE · WEEKLY AMOUNT

SECURITY HYGIENE

- ☐ Seed offline
- ☐ 2FA on
- ☐ Hardware wallet
- ☐ Multi-sig
- ☐ Tested recovery
- ☐ No screenshots

MACRO · ON-CHAIN METRICS · THE CYCLE STAGE

Next thesis check · unlock event: ______

Crypto Log

on-chain · DCA · the long-term thesis

Wallet · cold / hot: ______ Today · trade #: ______

TRADES

Date	Coin	Side	Entry	Exit	Qty	PnL

COLD STORAGE · SEED BACKED UP?

HOT WALLET · GAS FEES THIS WEEK

THESIS · WHY THIS COIN

DCA SCHEDULE · WEEKLY AMOUNT

SECURITY HYGIENE

- ☐ Seed offline
- ☐ 2FA on
- ☐ Hardware wallet
- ☐ Multi-sig
- ☐ Tested recovery
- ☐ No screenshots

MACRO · ON-CHAIN METRICS · THE CYCLE STAGE

Next thesis check · unlock event: ______

Crypto Log

on-chain · DCA · the long-term thesis

Wallet · cold / hot: ______ Today · trade #: _____

TRADES

Date	Coin	Side	Entry	Exit	Qty	PnL

COLD STORAGE · SEED BACKED UP?

HOT WALLET · GAS FEES THIS WEEK

THESIS · WHY THIS COIN

DCA SCHEDULE · WEEKLY AMOUNT

SECURITY HYGIENE

- ☐ Seed offline
- ☐ 2FA on
- ☐ Hardware wallet
- ☐ Multi-sig
- ☐ Tested recovery
- ☐ No screenshots

MACRO · ON-CHAIN METRICS · THE CYCLE STAGE

Next thesis check · unlock event: ______

Crypto Log

on-chain · DCA · the long-term thesis

Wallet · cold / hot: ______ Today · trade #: ______

TRADES

Date	Coin	Side	Entry	Exit	Qty	PnL

COLD STORAGE · SEED BACKED UP?

HOT WALLET · GAS FEES THIS WEEK

THESIS · WHY THIS COIN

DCA SCHEDULE · WEEKLY AMOUNT

SECURITY HYGIENE

- ☐ Seed offline
- ☐ 2FA on
- ☐ Hardware wallet
- ☐ Multi-sig
- ☐ Tested recovery
- ☐ No screenshots

MACRO · ON-CHAIN METRICS · THE CYCLE STAGE

Next thesis check · unlock event: ______

Crypto Log

on-chain · DCA · the long-term thesis

Wallet · cold / hot: ______ Today · trade #: _____

TRADES

Date	Coin	Side	Entry	Exit	Qty	PnL

COLD STORAGE · SEED BACKED UP?

HOT WALLET · GAS FEES THIS WEEK

THESIS · WHY THIS COIN

DCA SCHEDULE · WEEKLY AMOUNT

SECURITY HYGIENE

☐ Seed offline
☐ 2FA on
☐ Hardware wallet
☐ Multi-sig
☐ Tested recovery
☐ No screenshots

MACRO · ON-CHAIN METRICS · THE CYCLE STAGE

Next thesis check · unlock event:

Crypto Log

on-chain · DCA · the long-term thesis

Wallet · cold / hot: ______ Today · trade #: ______

TRADES

Date	Coin	Side	Entry	Exit	Qty	PnL

COLD STORAGE · SEED BACKED UP?

HOT WALLET · GAS FEES THIS WEEK

THESIS · WHY THIS COIN

DCA SCHEDULE · WEEKLY AMOUNT

SECURITY HYGIENE

- ☐ Seed offline
- ☐ 2FA on
- ☐ Hardware wallet
- ☐ Multi-sig
- ☐ Tested recovery
- ☐ No screenshots

MACRO · ON-CHAIN METRICS · THE CYCLE STAGE

Next thesis check · unlock event: ______

Crypto Log

on-chain · DCA · the long-term thesis

Wallet · cold / hot: ______ Today · trade #: ______

TRADES

Date	Coin	Side	Entry	Exit	Qty	PnL

COLD STORAGE · SEED BACKED UP?

HOT WALLET · GAS FEES THIS WEEK

THESIS · WHY THIS COIN

DCA SCHEDULE · WEEKLY AMOUNT

SECURITY HYGIENE

- ☐ Seed offline
- ☐ 2FA on
- ☐ Hardware wallet
- ☐ Multi-sig
- ☐ Tested recovery
- ☐ No screenshots

MACRO · ON-CHAIN METRICS · THE CYCLE STAGE

Next thesis check · unlock event: ______

Crypto Log

on-chain · DCA · the long-term thesis

Wallet · cold / hot: ______ Today · trade #: ______

TRADES

Date	Coin	Side	Entry	Exit	Qty	PnL

COLD STORAGE · SEED BACKED UP?

HOT WALLET · GAS FEES THIS WEEK

THESIS · WHY THIS COIN

DCA SCHEDULE · WEEKLY AMOUNT

SECURITY HYGIENE

- ☐ Seed offline
- ☐ 2FA on
- ☐ Hardware wallet
- ☐ Multi-sig
- ☐ Tested recovery
- ☐ No screenshots

MACRO · ON-CHAIN METRICS · THE CYCLE STAGE

Next thesis check · unlock event: ______

Crypto Log

on-chain · DCA · the long-term thesis

Wallet · cold / hot: ______ Today · trade #: _____

TRADES

Date	Coin	Side	Entry	Exit	Qty	PnL

COLD STORAGE · SEED BACKED UP?

HOT WALLET · GAS FEES THIS WEEK

THESIS · WHY THIS COIN

DCA SCHEDULE · WEEKLY AMOUNT

SECURITY HYGIENE

- ☐ Seed offline
- ☐ 2FA on
- ☐ Hardware wallet
- ☐ Multi-sig
- ☐ Tested recovery
- ☐ No screenshots

MACRO · ON-CHAIN METRICS · THE CYCLE STAGE

Next thesis check · unlock event: ____________

Crypto Log

on-chain · DCA · the long-term thesis

Wallet · cold / hot: ______ Today · trade #: _____

TRADES

Date	Coin	Side	Entry	Exit	Qty	PnL

COLD STORAGE · SEED BACKED UP?

HOT WALLET · GAS FEES THIS WEEK

THESIS · WHY THIS COIN

DCA SCHEDULE · WEEKLY AMOUNT

SECURITY HYGIENE

- ☐ Seed offline
- ☐ 2FA on
- ☐ Hardware wallet
- ☐ Multi-sig
- ☐ Tested recovery
- ☐ No screenshots

MACRO · ON-CHAIN METRICS · THE CYCLE STAGE

Next thesis check · unlock event: ______

Crypto Log

on-chain · DCA · the long-term thesis

Wallet · cold / hot: ______ Today · trade #: ______

TRADES

Date	Coin	Side	Entry	Exit	Qty	PnL

COLD STORAGE · SEED BACKED UP?

HOT WALLET · GAS FEES THIS WEEK

THESIS · WHY THIS COIN

DCA SCHEDULE · WEEKLY AMOUNT

SECURITY HYGIENE

- ☐ Seed offline
- ☐ 2FA on
- ☐ Hardware wallet
- ☐ Multi-sig
- ☐ Tested recovery
- ☐ No screenshots

MACRO · ON-CHAIN METRICS · THE CYCLE STAGE

Next thesis check · unlock event: ______

Crypto Log

on-chain · DCA · the long-term thesis

Wallet · cold / hot: ______ Today · trade #: _____

TRADES

Date	Coin	Side	Entry	Exit	Qty	PnL

COLD STORAGE · SEED BACKED UP?

HOT WALLET · GAS FEES THIS WEEK

THESIS · WHY THIS COIN

DCA SCHEDULE · WEEKLY AMOUNT

SECURITY HYGIENE

- ☐ Seed offline
- ☐ 2FA on
- ☐ Hardware wallet
- ☐ Multi-sig
- ☐ Tested recovery
- ☐ No screenshots

MACRO · ON-CHAIN METRICS · THE CYCLE STAGE

Next thesis check · unlock event: ______

Crypto Log

on-chain · DCA · the long-term thesis

Wallet · cold / hot: ______ Today · trade #: _____

TRADES

Date	Coin	Side	Entry	Exit	Qty	PnL

COLD STORAGE · SEED BACKED UP?

HOT WALLET · GAS FEES THIS WEEK

THESIS · WHY THIS COIN

DCA SCHEDULE · WEEKLY AMOUNT

SECURITY HYGIENE

- ☐ Seed offline
- ☐ 2FA on
- ☐ Hardware wallet
- ☐ Multi-sig
- ☐ Tested recovery
- ☐ No screenshots

MACRO · ON-CHAIN METRICS · THE CYCLE STAGE

Next thesis check · unlock event: ______

Crypto Log

on-chain · DCA · the long-term thesis

Wallet · cold / hot: ______ Today · trade #: ______

TRADES

Date	Coin	Side	Entry	Exit	Qty	PnL

COLD STORAGE · SEED BACKED UP?

HOT WALLET · GAS FEES THIS WEEK

THESIS · WHY THIS COIN

DCA SCHEDULE · WEEKLY AMOUNT

SECURITY HYGIENE

- ☐ Seed offline
- ☐ 2FA on
- ☐ Hardware wallet
- ☐ Multi-sig
- ☐ Tested recovery
- ☐ No screenshots

MACRO · ON-CHAIN METRICS · THE CYCLE STAGE

Next thesis check · unlock event: ______

Crypto Log

on-chain · DCA · the long-term thesis

Wallet · cold / hot: ______ Today · trade #: _____

TRADES

Date	Coin	Side	Entry	Exit	Qty	PnL

COLD STORAGE · SEED BACKED UP?

HOT WALLET · GAS FEES THIS WEEK

THESIS · WHY THIS COIN

DCA SCHEDULE · WEEKLY AMOUNT

SECURITY HYGIENE

- ☐ Seed offline
- ☐ 2FA on
- ☐ Hardware wallet
- ☐ Multi-sig
- ☐ Tested recovery
- ☐ No screenshots

MACRO · ON-CHAIN METRICS · THE CYCLE STAGE

Next thesis check · unlock event: ____

Crypto Log

on-chain · DCA · the long-term thesis

Wallet · cold / hot: ______ Today · trade #: ______

TRADES

Date	Coin	Side	Entry	Exit	Qty	PnL

COLD STORAGE · SEED BACKED UP?

HOT WALLET · GAS FEES THIS WEEK

THESIS · WHY THIS COIN

DCA SCHEDULE · WEEKLY AMOUNT

SECURITY HYGIENE

- ☐ Seed offline
- ☐ 2FA on
- ☐ Hardware wallet
- ☐ Multi-sig
- ☐ Tested recovery
- ☐ No screenshots

MACRO · ON-CHAIN METRICS · THE CYCLE STAGE

Next thesis check · unlock event:

Crypto Log

on-chain · DCA · the long-term thesis

Wallet · cold / hot: ______ Today · trade #: _____

TRADES

Date	Coin	Side	Entry	Exit	Qty	PnL

COLD STORAGE · SEED BACKED UP?

HOT WALLET · GAS FEES THIS WEEK

THESIS · WHY THIS COIN

DCA SCHEDULE · WEEKLY AMOUNT

SECURITY HYGIENE

- ☐ Seed offline
- ☐ 2FA on
- ☐ Hardware wallet
- ☐ Multi-sig
- ☐ Tested recovery
- ☐ No screenshots

MACRO · ON-CHAIN METRICS · THE CYCLE STAGE

Next thesis check · unlock event:

Crypto Log

on-chain · DCA · the long-term thesis

Wallet · cold / hot: ______ Today · trade #: ______

TRADES

Date	Coin	Side	Entry	Exit	Qty	PnL

COLD STORAGE · SEED BACKED UP?

HOT WALLET · GAS FEES THIS WEEK

THESIS · WHY THIS COIN

DCA SCHEDULE · WEEKLY AMOUNT

SECURITY HYGIENE

- ☐ Seed offline
- ☐ 2FA on
- ☐ Hardware wallet
- ☐ Multi-sig
- ☐ Tested recovery
- ☐ No screenshots

MACRO · ON-CHAIN METRICS · THE CYCLE STAGE

Next thesis check · unlock event: ______

Crypto Log

on-chain · DCA · the long-term thesis

Wallet · cold / hot: ______ Today · trade #: _____

TRADES

Date	Coin	Side	Entry	Exit	Qty	PnL

COLD STORAGE · SEED BACKED UP?

HOT WALLET · GAS FEES THIS WEEK

THESIS · WHY THIS COIN

DCA SCHEDULE · WEEKLY AMOUNT

SECURITY HYGIENE

- ☐ Seed offline
- ☐ 2FA on
- ☐ Hardware wallet
- ☐ Multi-sig
- ☐ Tested recovery
- ☐ No screenshots

MACRO · ON-CHAIN METRICS · THE CYCLE STAGE

Next thesis check · unlock event: ______

Crypto Log

on-chain · DCA · the long-term thesis

Wallet · cold / hot: ______ Today · trade #: ______

TRADES

Date	Coin	Side	Entry	Exit	Qty	PnL

COLD STORAGE · SEED BACKED UP?

HOT WALLET · GAS FEES THIS WEEK

THESIS · WHY THIS COIN

DCA SCHEDULE · WEEKLY AMOUNT

SECURITY HYGIENE

- ☐ Seed offline
- ☐ 2FA on
- ☐ Hardware wallet
- ☐ Multi-sig
- ☐ Tested recovery
- ☐ No screenshots

MACRO · ON-CHAIN METRICS · THE CYCLE STAGE

Next thesis check · unlock event: ______

Crypto Log

on-chain · DCA · the long-term thesis

Wallet · cold / hot: ______ Today · trade #: _____

TRADES

Date	Coin	Side	Entry	Exit	Qty	PnL

COLD STORAGE · SEED BACKED UP?

HOT WALLET · GAS FEES THIS WEEK

THESIS · WHY THIS COIN

DCA SCHEDULE · WEEKLY AMOUNT

SECURITY HYGIENE

- ☐ Seed offline
- ☐ 2FA on
- ☐ Hardware wallet
- ☐ Multi-sig
- ☐ Tested recovery
- ☐ No screenshots

MACRO · ON-CHAIN METRICS · THE CYCLE STAGE

Next thesis check · unlock event: ______

Crypto Log

on-chain · DCA · the long-term thesis

Wallet · cold / hot: ______ Today · trade #: ______

TRADES

Date	Coin	Side	Entry	Exit	Qty	PnL

COLD STORAGE · SEED BACKED UP?

HOT WALLET · GAS FEES THIS WEEK

THESIS · WHY THIS COIN

DCA SCHEDULE · WEEKLY AMOUNT

SECURITY HYGIENE

- ☐ Seed offline
- ☐ 2FA on
- ☐ Hardware wallet
- ☐ Multi-sig
- ☐ Tested recovery
- ☐ No screenshots

MACRO · ON-CHAIN METRICS · THE CYCLE STAGE

Next thesis check · unlock event: ______

Crypto Log

on-chain · DCA · the long-term thesis

Wallet · cold / hot: ______ Today · trade #: ______

TRADES

Date	Coin	Side	Entry	Exit	Qty	PnL

COLD STORAGE · SEED BACKED UP?

HOT WALLET · GAS FEES THIS WEEK

THESIS · WHY THIS COIN

DCA SCHEDULE · WEEKLY AMOUNT

SECURITY HYGIENE

- ☐ Seed offline
- ☐ 2FA on
- ☐ Hardware wallet
- ☐ Multi-sig
- ☐ Tested recovery
- ☐ No screenshots

MACRO · ON-CHAIN METRICS · THE CYCLE STAGE

Next thesis check · unlock event: ______

Crypto Log

on-chain · DCA · the long-term thesis

Wallet · cold / hot: ______ Today · trade #: ______

TRADES

Date	Coin	Side	Entry	Exit	Qty	PnL

COLD STORAGE · SEED BACKED UP?

HOT WALLET · GAS FEES THIS WEEK

THESIS · WHY THIS COIN

DCA SCHEDULE · WEEKLY AMOUNT

SECURITY HYGIENE

- ☐ Seed offline
- ☐ 2FA on
- ☐ Hardware wallet
- ☐ Multi-sig
- ☐ Tested recovery
- ☐ No screenshots

MACRO · ON-CHAIN METRICS · THE CYCLE STAGE

Next thesis check · unlock event: ______

Crypto Log

on-chain · DCA · the long-term thesis

Wallet · cold / hot: ______ Today · trade #: _____

TRADES

Date	Coin	Side	Entry	Exit	Qty	PnL

COLD STORAGE · SEED BACKED UP?

HOT WALLET · GAS FEES THIS WEEK

THESIS · WHY THIS COIN

DCA SCHEDULE · WEEKLY AMOUNT

SECURITY HYGIENE

☐ Seed offline
☐ 2FA on
☐ Hardware wallet
☐ Multi-sig
☐ Tested recovery
☐ No screenshots

MACRO · ON-CHAIN METRICS · THE CYCLE STAGE

Next thesis check · unlock event: ____________

Crypto Log

on-chain · DCA · the long-term thesis

Wallet · cold / hot: ______ Today · trade #: ______

TRADES

Date	Coin	Side	Entry	Exit	Qty	PnL

COLD STORAGE · SEED BACKED UP?

HOT WALLET · GAS FEES THIS WEEK

THESIS · WHY THIS COIN

DCA SCHEDULE · WEEKLY AMOUNT

SECURITY HYGIENE

- ☐ Seed offline
- ☐ 2FA on
- ☐ Hardware wallet
- ☐ Multi-sig
- ☐ Tested recovery
- ☐ No screenshots

MACRO · ON-CHAIN METRICS · THE CYCLE STAGE

Next thesis check · unlock event: ______

Crypto Log

on-chain · DCA · the long-term thesis

Wallet · cold / hot: ______ Today · trade #: _____

TRADES

Date	Coin	Side	Entry	Exit	Qty	PnL

COLD STORAGE · SEED BACKED UP?

HOT WALLET · GAS FEES THIS WEEK

THESIS · WHY THIS COIN

DCA SCHEDULE · WEEKLY AMOUNT

SECURITY HYGIENE

- ☐ Seed offline
- ☐ 2FA on
- ☐ Hardware wallet
- ☐ Multi-sig
- ☐ Tested recovery
- ☐ No screenshots

MACRO · ON-CHAIN METRICS · THE CYCLE STAGE

Next thesis check · unlock event: ____________

Crypto Log

on-chain · DCA · the long-term thesis

Wallet · cold / hot: ______ Today · trade #: ______

TRADES

Date	Coin	Side	Entry	Exit	Qty	PnL

COLD STORAGE · SEED BACKED UP?

HOT WALLET · GAS FEES THIS WEEK

THESIS · WHY THIS COIN

DCA SCHEDULE · WEEKLY AMOUNT

SECURITY HYGIENE

- ☐ Seed offline
- ☐ 2FA on
- ☐ Hardware wallet
- ☐ Multi-sig
- ☐ Tested recovery
- ☐ No screenshots

MACRO · ON-CHAIN METRICS · THE CYCLE STAGE

Next thesis check · unlock event: ______

Crypto Log

on-chain · DCA · the long-term thesis

Wallet · cold / hot: ______ Today · trade #: _____

TRADES

Date	Coin	Side	Entry	Exit	Qty	PnL

COLD STORAGE · SEED BACKED UP?

HOT WALLET · GAS FEES THIS WEEK

THESIS · WHY THIS COIN

DCA SCHEDULE · WEEKLY AMOUNT

SECURITY HYGIENE

- ☐ Seed offline
- ☐ 2FA on
- ☐ Hardware wallet
- ☐ Multi-sig
- ☐ Tested recovery
- ☐ No screenshots

MACRO · ON-CHAIN METRICS · THE CYCLE STAGE

Next thesis check · unlock event: ______

Crypto Log

on-chain · DCA · the long-term thesis

Wallet · cold / hot: ______ Today · trade #: ______

TRADES

Date	Coin	Side	Entry	Exit	Qty	PnL

COLD STORAGE · SEED BACKED UP?

HOT WALLET · GAS FEES THIS WEEK

THESIS · WHY THIS COIN

DCA SCHEDULE · WEEKLY AMOUNT

SECURITY HYGIENE

- ☐ Seed offline
- ☐ 2FA on
- ☐ Hardware wallet
- ☐ Multi-sig
- ☐ Tested recovery
- ☐ No screenshots

MACRO · ON-CHAIN METRICS · THE CYCLE STAGE

Next thesis check · unlock event: ______

Crypto Log

on-chain · DCA · the long-term thesis

Wallet · cold / hot: ______ Today · trade #: _____

TRADES

Date	Coin	Side	Entry	Exit	Qty	PnL

COLD STORAGE · SEED BACKED UP?

HOT WALLET · GAS FEES THIS WEEK

THESIS · WHY THIS COIN

DCA SCHEDULE · WEEKLY AMOUNT

SECURITY HYGIENE

- ☐ Seed offline
- ☐ 2FA on
- ☐ Hardware wallet
- ☐ Multi-sig
- ☐ Tested recovery
- ☐ No screenshots

MACRO · ON-CHAIN METRICS · THE CYCLE STAGE

Next thesis check · unlock event: ______

Crypto Log

on-chain · DCA · the long-term thesis

Wallet · cold / hot: ______ Today · trade #: ______

TRADES

Date	Coin	Side	Entry	Exit	Qty	PnL

COLD STORAGE · SEED BACKED UP?

HOT WALLET · GAS FEES THIS WEEK

THESIS · WHY THIS COIN

DCA SCHEDULE · WEEKLY AMOUNT

SECURITY HYGIENE

- ☐ Seed offline
- ☐ 2FA on
- ☐ Hardware wallet
- ☐ Multi-sig
- ☐ Tested recovery
- ☐ No screenshots

MACRO · ON-CHAIN METRICS · THE CYCLE STAGE

Next thesis check · unlock event: ______

Crypto Log

on-chain · DCA · the long-term thesis

Wallet · cold / hot: ______ Today · trade #: ______

TRADES

Date	Coin	Side	Entry	Exit	Qty	PnL

COLD STORAGE · SEED BACKED UP?

HOT WALLET · GAS FEES THIS WEEK

THESIS · WHY THIS COIN

DCA SCHEDULE · WEEKLY AMOUNT

SECURITY HYGIENE

- ☐ Seed offline
- ☐ 2FA on
- ☐ Hardware wallet
- ☐ Multi-sig
- ☐ Tested recovery
- ☐ No screenshots

MACRO · ON-CHAIN METRICS · THE CYCLE STAGE

Next thesis check · unlock event: ______

Crypto Log

on-chain · DCA · the long-term thesis

Wallet · cold / hot: ______ Today · trade #: _____

TRADES

Date	Coin	Side	Entry	Exit	Qty	PnL

COLD STORAGE · SEED BACKED UP?

HOT WALLET · GAS FEES THIS WEEK

THESIS · WHY THIS COIN

DCA SCHEDULE · WEEKLY AMOUNT

SECURITY HYGIENE

- ☐ Seed offline
- ☐ 2FA on
- ☐ Hardware wallet
- ☐ Multi-sig
- ☐ Tested recovery
- ☐ No screenshots

MACRO · ON-CHAIN METRICS · THE CYCLE STAGE

Next thesis check · unlock event: ______

Crypto Log

on-chain · DCA · the long-term thesis

Wallet · cold / hot: ______ Today · trade #: _____

TRADES

Date	Coin	Side	Entry	Exit	Qty	PnL

COLD STORAGE · SEED BACKED UP?

HOT WALLET · GAS FEES THIS WEEK

THESIS · WHY THIS COIN

DCA SCHEDULE · WEEKLY AMOUNT

SECURITY HYGIENE

- ☐ Seed offline
- ☐ 2FA on
- ☐ Hardware wallet
- ☐ Multi-sig
- ☐ Tested recovery
- ☐ No screenshots

MACRO · ON-CHAIN METRICS · THE CYCLE STAGE

Next thesis check · unlock event: ______

Crypto Log

on-chain · DCA · the long-term thesis

Wallet · cold / hot: ______ Today · trade #: _____

TRADES

Date	Coin	Side	Entry	Exit	Qty	PnL

COLD STORAGE · SEED BACKED UP?

HOT WALLET · GAS FEES THIS WEEK

THESIS · WHY THIS COIN

DCA SCHEDULE · WEEKLY AMOUNT

SECURITY HYGIENE

- ☐ Seed offline
- ☐ 2FA on
- ☐ Hardware wallet
- ☐ Multi-sig
- ☐ Tested recovery
- ☐ No screenshots

MACRO · ON-CHAIN METRICS · THE CYCLE STAGE

Next thesis check · unlock event: ______

Crypto Log

on-chain · DCA · the long-term thesis

Wallet · cold / hot: ______ Today · trade #: _____

TRADES

Date	Coin	Side	Entry	Exit	Qty	PnL

COLD STORAGE · SEED BACKED UP?

HOT WALLET · GAS FEES THIS WEEK

THESIS · WHY THIS COIN

DCA SCHEDULE · WEEKLY AMOUNT

SECURITY HYGIENE

- ☐ Seed offline
- ☐ 2FA on
- ☐ Hardware wallet
- ☐ Multi-sig
- ☐ Tested recovery
- ☐ No screenshots

MACRO · ON-CHAIN METRICS · THE CYCLE STAGE

Next thesis check · unlock event: ______

Crypto Log

on-chain · DCA · the long-term thesis

Wallet · cold / hot: ______ Today · trade #: ______

TRADES

Date	Coin	Side	Entry	Exit	Qty	PnL

COLD STORAGE · SEED BACKED UP?

HOT WALLET · GAS FEES THIS WEEK

THESIS · WHY THIS COIN

DCA SCHEDULE · WEEKLY AMOUNT

SECURITY HYGIENE

- ☐ Seed offline
- ☐ 2FA on
- ☐ Hardware wallet
- ☐ Multi-sig
- ☐ Tested recovery
- ☐ No screenshots

MACRO · ON-CHAIN METRICS · THE CYCLE STAGE

Next thesis check · unlock event: ______

Crypto Log

on-chain · DCA · the long-term thesis

Wallet · cold / hot: ______ Today · trade #: _____

TRADES

Date	Coin	Side	Entry	Exit	Qty	PnL

COLD STORAGE · SEED BACKED UP?

HOT WALLET · GAS FEES THIS WEEK

THESIS · WHY THIS COIN

DCA SCHEDULE · WEEKLY AMOUNT

SECURITY HYGIENE

- ☐ Seed offline
- ☐ 2FA on
- ☐ Hardware wallet
- ☐ Multi-sig
- ☐ Tested recovery
- ☐ No screenshots

MACRO · ON-CHAIN METRICS · THE CYCLE STAGE

Next thesis check · unlock event: ______

Crypto Log

on-chain · DCA · the long-term thesis

Wallet · cold / hot: ______ Today · trade #: _____

TRADES

Date	Coin	Side	Entry	Exit	Qty	PnL

COLD STORAGE · SEED BACKED UP?

HOT WALLET · GAS FEES THIS WEEK

THESIS · WHY THIS COIN

DCA SCHEDULE · WEEKLY AMOUNT

SECURITY HYGIENE

- ☐ Seed offline
- ☐ 2FA on
- ☐ Hardware wallet
- ☐ Multi-sig
- ☐ Tested recovery
- ☐ No screenshots

MACRO · ON-CHAIN METRICS · THE CYCLE STAGE

Next thesis check · unlock event: ______

Crypto Log

on-chain · DCA · the long-term thesis

Wallet · cold / hot: ______ Today · trade #: _____

TRADES

Date	Coin	Side	Entry	Exit	Qty	PnL

COLD STORAGE · SEED BACKED UP?

HOT WALLET · GAS FEES THIS WEEK

THESIS · WHY THIS COIN

DCA SCHEDULE · WEEKLY AMOUNT

SECURITY HYGIENE

- ☐ Seed offline
- ☐ 2FA on
- ☐ Hardware wallet
- ☐ Multi-sig
- ☐ Tested recovery
- ☐ No screenshots

MACRO · ON-CHAIN METRICS · THE CYCLE STAGE

Next thesis check · unlock event: ______

Crypto Log

on-chain · DCA · the long-term thesis

Wallet · cold / hot: ______ Today · trade #: ______

TRADES

Date	Coin	Side	Entry	Exit	Qty	PnL

COLD STORAGE · SEED BACKED UP?

HOT WALLET · GAS FEES THIS WEEK

THESIS · WHY THIS COIN

DCA SCHEDULE · WEEKLY AMOUNT

SECURITY HYGIENE

- ☐ Seed offline
- ☐ 2FA on
- ☐ Hardware wallet
- ☐ Multi-sig
- ☐ Tested recovery
- ☐ No screenshots

MACRO · ON-CHAIN METRICS · THE CYCLE STAGE

Next thesis check · unlock event: ______

Crypto Log

on-chain · DCA · the long-term thesis

Wallet · cold / hot: ______ Today · trade #: _____

TRADES

Date	Coin	Side	Entry	Exit	Qty	PnL

COLD STORAGE · SEED BACKED UP?

HOT WALLET · GAS FEES THIS WEEK

THESIS · WHY THIS COIN

DCA SCHEDULE · WEEKLY AMOUNT

SECURITY HYGIENE

- ☐ Seed offline
- ☐ 2FA on
- ☐ Hardware wallet
- ☐ Multi-sig
- ☐ Tested recovery
- ☐ No screenshots

MACRO · ON-CHAIN METRICS · THE CYCLE STAGE

Next thesis check · unlock event: ______

Crypto Log

on-chain · DCA · the long-term thesis

Wallet · cold / hot: ______ Today · trade #: ______

TRADES

Date	Coin	Side	Entry	Exit	Qty	PnL

COLD STORAGE · SEED BACKED UP?

HOT WALLET · GAS FEES THIS WEEK

THESIS · WHY THIS COIN

DCA SCHEDULE · WEEKLY AMOUNT

SECURITY HYGIENE

- ☐ Seed offline
- ☐ 2FA on
- ☐ Hardware wallet
- ☐ Multi-sig
- ☐ Tested recovery
- ☐ No screenshots

MACRO · ON-CHAIN METRICS · THE CYCLE STAGE

Next thesis check · unlock event: ______

Crypto Log

on-chain · DCA · the long-term thesis

Wallet · cold / hot: ______ Today · trade #: ______

TRADES

Date	Coin	Side	Entry	Exit	Qty	PnL

COLD STORAGE · SEED BACKED UP?

HOT WALLET · GAS FEES THIS WEEK

THESIS · WHY THIS COIN

DCA SCHEDULE · WEEKLY AMOUNT

SECURITY HYGIENE

- ☐ Seed offline
- ☐ 2FA on
- ☐ Hardware wallet
- ☐ Multi-sig
- ☐ Tested recovery
- ☐ No screenshots

MACRO · ON-CHAIN METRICS · THE CYCLE STAGE

Next thesis check · unlock event: ______

Crypto Log

on-chain · DCA · the long-term thesis

Wallet · cold / hot: ______ Today · trade #: ______

TRADES

Date	Coin	Side	Entry	Exit	Qty	PnL

COLD STORAGE · SEED BACKED UP?

HOT WALLET · GAS FEES THIS WEEK

THESIS · WHY THIS COIN

DCA SCHEDULE · WEEKLY AMOUNT

SECURITY HYGIENE

- ☐ Seed offline
- ☐ 2FA on
- ☐ Hardware wallet
- ☐ Multi-sig
- ☐ Tested recovery
- ☐ No screenshots

MACRO · ON-CHAIN METRICS · THE CYCLE STAGE

Next thesis check · unlock event: ______

Crypto Log

on-chain · DCA · the long-term thesis

Wallet · cold / hot: ______ Today · trade #: ______

TRADES

Date	Coin	Side	Entry	Exit	Qty	PnL

COLD STORAGE · SEED BACKED UP?

HOT WALLET · GAS FEES THIS WEEK

THESIS · WHY THIS COIN

DCA SCHEDULE · WEEKLY AMOUNT

SECURITY HYGIENE

- ☐ Seed offline
- ☐ 2FA on
- ☐ Hardware wallet
- ☐ Multi-sig
- ☐ Tested recovery
- ☐ No screenshots

MACRO · ON-CHAIN METRICS · THE CYCLE STAGE

Next thesis check · unlock event: ______

Crypto Log

on-chain · DCA · the long-term thesis

Wallet · cold / hot: ______ Today · trade #: ______

TRADES

Date	Coin	Side	Entry	Exit	Qty	PnL

COLD STORAGE · SEED BACKED UP?

HOT WALLET · GAS FEES THIS WEEK

THESIS · WHY THIS COIN

DCA SCHEDULE · WEEKLY AMOUNT

SECURITY HYGIENE

- ☐ Seed offline
- ☐ 2FA on
- ☐ Hardware wallet
- ☐ Multi-sig
- ☐ Tested recovery
- ☐ No screenshots

MACRO · ON-CHAIN METRICS · THE CYCLE STAGE

Next thesis check · unlock event: ______

Crypto Log

on-chain · DCA · the long-term thesis

Wallet · cold / hot: ______ Today · trade #: _____

TRADES

Date	Coin	Side	Entry	Exit	Qty	PnL

COLD STORAGE · SEED BACKED UP?

HOT WALLET · GAS FEES THIS WEEK

THESIS · WHY THIS COIN

DCA SCHEDULE · WEEKLY AMOUNT

SECURITY HYGIENE

- ☐ Seed offline
- ☐ 2FA on
- ☐ Hardware wallet
- ☐ Multi-sig
- ☐ Tested recovery
- ☐ No screenshots

MACRO · ON-CHAIN METRICS · THE CYCLE STAGE

Next thesis check · unlock event: ____________

Crypto Log

on-chain · DCA · the long-term thesis

Wallet · cold / hot: ______ Today · trade #: ______

TRADES

Date	Coin	Side	Entry	Exit	Qty	PnL

COLD STORAGE · SEED BACKED UP?

HOT WALLET · GAS FEES THIS WEEK

THESIS · WHY THIS COIN

DCA SCHEDULE · WEEKLY AMOUNT

SECURITY HYGIENE

- ☐ Seed offline
- ☐ 2FA on
- ☐ Hardware wallet
- ☐ Multi-sig
- ☐ Tested recovery
- ☐ No screenshots

MACRO · ON-CHAIN METRICS · THE CYCLE STAGE

Next thesis check · unlock event: ______

Crypto Log

on-chain · DCA · the long-term thesis

Wallet · cold / hot: ______ Today · trade #: ______

TRADES

Date	Coin	Side	Entry	Exit	Qty	PnL

COLD STORAGE · SEED BACKED UP?

HOT WALLET · GAS FEES THIS WEEK

THESIS · WHY THIS COIN

DCA SCHEDULE · WEEKLY AMOUNT

SECURITY HYGIENE

- ☐ Seed offline
- ☐ 2FA on
- ☐ Hardware wallet
- ☐ Multi-sig
- ☐ Tested recovery
- ☐ No screenshots

MACRO · ON-CHAIN METRICS · THE CYCLE STAGE

Next thesis check · unlock event: ______

Crypto Log

on-chain · DCA · the long-term thesis

Wallet · cold / hot: ______ Today · trade #: ______

TRADES

Date	Coin	Side	Entry	Exit	Qty	PnL

COLD STORAGE · SEED BACKED UP?

HOT WALLET · GAS FEES THIS WEEK

THESIS · WHY THIS COIN

DCA SCHEDULE · WEEKLY AMOUNT

SECURITY HYGIENE

- ☐ Seed offline
- ☐ 2FA on
- ☐ Hardware wallet
- ☐ Multi-sig
- ☐ Tested recovery
- ☐ No screenshots

MACRO · ON-CHAIN METRICS · THE CYCLE STAGE

Next thesis check · unlock event:

Crypto Log

on-chain · DCA · the long-term thesis

Wallet · cold / hot: ______ Today · trade #: _____

TRADES

Date	Coin	Side	Entry	Exit	Qty	PnL

COLD STORAGE · SEED BACKED UP?

HOT WALLET · GAS FEES THIS WEEK

THESIS · WHY THIS COIN

DCA SCHEDULE · WEEKLY AMOUNT

SECURITY HYGIENE

- ☐ Seed offline
- ☐ 2FA on
- ☐ Hardware wallet
- ☐ Multi-sig
- ☐ Tested recovery
- ☐ No screenshots

MACRO · ON-CHAIN METRICS · THE CYCLE STAGE

Next thesis check · unlock event:

Crypto Log

on-chain · DCA · the long-term thesis

Wallet · cold / hot: ______ Today · trade #: ______

TRADES

Date	Coin	Side	Entry	Exit	Qty	PnL

COLD STORAGE · SEED BACKED UP?

HOT WALLET · GAS FEES THIS WEEK

THESIS · WHY THIS COIN

DCA SCHEDULE · WEEKLY AMOUNT

SECURITY HYGIENE

- ☐ Seed offline
- ☐ 2FA on
- ☐ Hardware wallet
- ☐ Multi-sig
- ☐ Tested recovery
- ☐ No screenshots

MACRO · ON-CHAIN METRICS · THE CYCLE STAGE

Next thesis check · unlock event: ______

Crypto Log

on-chain · DCA · the long-term thesis

Wallet · cold / hot: ______ Today · trade #: _____

TRADES

Date	Coin	Side	Entry	Exit	Qty	PnL

COLD STORAGE · SEED BACKED UP?

HOT WALLET · GAS FEES THIS WEEK

THESIS · WHY THIS COIN

DCA SCHEDULE · WEEKLY AMOUNT

SECURITY HYGIENE

- ☐ Seed offline
- ☐ 2FA on
- ☐ Hardware wallet
- ☐ Multi-sig
- ☐ Tested recovery
- ☐ No screenshots

MACRO · ON-CHAIN METRICS · THE CYCLE STAGE

Next thesis check · unlock event: ______

Crypto Log

on-chain · DCA · the long-term thesis

Wallet · cold / hot: ______ Today · trade #: ______

TRADES

Date	Coin	Side	Entry	Exit	Qty	PnL

COLD STORAGE · SEED BACKED UP?

HOT WALLET · GAS FEES THIS WEEK

THESIS · WHY THIS COIN

DCA SCHEDULE · WEEKLY AMOUNT

SECURITY HYGIENE

- ☐ Seed offline
- ☐ 2FA on
- ☐ Hardware wallet
- ☐ Multi-sig
- ☐ Tested recovery
- ☐ No screenshots

MACRO · ON-CHAIN METRICS · THE CYCLE STAGE

Next thesis check · unlock event: ______

Crypto Log

on-chain · DCA · the long-term thesis

Wallet · cold / hot: ______ Today · trade #: _____

TRADES

Date	Coin	Side	Entry	Exit	Qty	PnL

COLD STORAGE · SEED BACKED UP?

HOT WALLET · GAS FEES THIS WEEK

THESIS · WHY THIS COIN

DCA SCHEDULE · WEEKLY AMOUNT

SECURITY HYGIENE

- ☐ Seed offline
- ☐ 2FA on
- ☐ Hardware wallet
- ☐ Multi-sig
- ☐ Tested recovery
- ☐ No screenshots

MACRO · ON-CHAIN METRICS · THE CYCLE STAGE

Next thesis check · unlock event: ______

Crypto Log

on-chain · DCA · the long-term thesis

Wallet · cold / hot: ______ Today · trade #: ______

TRADES

Date	Coin	Side	Entry	Exit	Qty	PnL

COLD STORAGE · SEED BACKED UP?

HOT WALLET · GAS FEES THIS WEEK

THESIS · WHY THIS COIN

DCA SCHEDULE · WEEKLY AMOUNT

SECURITY HYGIENE

- ☐ Seed offline
- ☐ 2FA on
- ☐ Hardware wallet
- ☐ Multi-sig
- ☐ Tested recovery
- ☐ No screenshots

MACRO · ON-CHAIN METRICS · THE CYCLE STAGE

Next thesis check · unlock event:

Crypto Log

on-chain · DCA · the long-term thesis

Wallet · cold / hot: ______ Today · trade #: ______

TRADES

Date	Coin	Side	Entry	Exit	Qty	PnL

COLD STORAGE · SEED BACKED UP?

HOT WALLET · GAS FEES THIS WEEK

THESIS · WHY THIS COIN

DCA SCHEDULE · WEEKLY AMOUNT

SECURITY HYGIENE

- ☐ Seed offline
- ☐ 2FA on
- ☐ Hardware wallet
- ☐ Multi-sig
- ☐ Tested recovery
- ☐ No screenshots

MACRO · ON-CHAIN METRICS · THE CYCLE STAGE

Next thesis check · unlock event: ______

Crypto Log

on-chain · DCA · the long-term thesis

Wallet · cold / hot: ______ Today · trade #: ______

TRADES

Date	Coin	Side	Entry	Exit	Qty	PnL

COLD STORAGE · SEED BACKED UP?

HOT WALLET · GAS FEES THIS WEEK

THESIS · WHY THIS COIN

DCA SCHEDULE · WEEKLY AMOUNT

SECURITY HYGIENE

- ☐ Seed offline
- ☐ 2FA on
- ☐ Hardware wallet
- ☐ Multi-sig
- ☐ Tested recovery
- ☐ No screenshots

MACRO · ON-CHAIN METRICS · THE CYCLE STAGE

Next thesis check · unlock event: ______

Crypto Log

on-chain · DCA · the long-term thesis

Wallet · cold / hot: ______ Today · trade #: _____

TRADES

Date	Coin	Side	Entry	Exit	Qty	PnL

COLD STORAGE · SEED BACKED UP?

HOT WALLET · GAS FEES THIS WEEK

THESIS · WHY THIS COIN

DCA SCHEDULE · WEEKLY AMOUNT

SECURITY HYGIENE

☐ Seed offline
☐ 2FA on
☐ Hardware wallet
☐ Multi-sig
☐ Tested recovery
☐ No screenshots

MACRO · ON-CHAIN METRICS · THE CYCLE STAGE

Next thesis check · unlock event: ______

Crypto Log

on-chain · DCA · the long-term thesis

Wallet · cold / hot: ______ Today · trade #: ______

TRADES

Date	Coin	Side	Entry	Exit	Qty	PnL

COLD STORAGE · SEED BACKED UP?

HOT WALLET · GAS FEES THIS WEEK

THESIS · WHY THIS COIN

DCA SCHEDULE · WEEKLY AMOUNT

SECURITY HYGIENE

- ☐ Seed offline
- ☐ 2FA on
- ☐ Hardware wallet
- ☐ Multi-sig
- ☐ Tested recovery
- ☐ No screenshots

MACRO · ON-CHAIN METRICS · THE CYCLE STAGE

Next thesis check · unlock event: ______

Crypto Log

on-chain · DCA · the long-term thesis

Wallet · cold / hot: ______ Today · trade #: _____

TRADES

Date	Coin	Side	Entry	Exit	Qty	PnL

COLD STORAGE · SEED BACKED UP?

HOT WALLET · GAS FEES THIS WEEK

THESIS · WHY THIS COIN

DCA SCHEDULE · WEEKLY AMOUNT

SECURITY HYGIENE

- ☐ Seed offline
- ☐ 2FA on
- ☐ Hardware wallet
- ☐ Multi-sig
- ☐ Tested recovery
- ☐ No screenshots

MACRO · ON-CHAIN METRICS · THE CYCLE STAGE

Next thesis check · unlock event: ______

Crypto Log

on-chain · DCA · the long-term thesis

Wallet · cold / hot: ______ Today · trade #: ______

TRADES

Date	Coin	Side	Entry	Exit	Qty	PnL

COLD STORAGE · SEED BACKED UP?

HOT WALLET · GAS FEES THIS WEEK

THESIS · WHY THIS COIN

DCA SCHEDULE · WEEKLY AMOUNT

SECURITY HYGIENE

- ☐ Seed offline
- ☐ 2FA on
- ☐ Hardware wallet
- ☐ Multi-sig
- ☐ Tested recovery
- ☐ No screenshots

MACRO · ON-CHAIN METRICS · THE CYCLE STAGE

Next thesis check · unlock event: ______

Crypto Log

on-chain · DCA · the long-term thesis

Wallet · cold / hot: ______ Today · trade #: _____

TRADES

Date	Coin	Side	Entry	Exit	Qty	PnL

COLD STORAGE · SEED BACKED UP?

HOT WALLET · GAS FEES THIS WEEK

THESIS · WHY THIS COIN

DCA SCHEDULE · WEEKLY AMOUNT

SECURITY HYGIENE

- ☐ Seed offline
- ☐ 2FA on
- ☐ Hardware wallet
- ☐ Multi-sig
- ☐ Tested recovery
- ☐ No screenshots

MACRO · ON-CHAIN METRICS · THE CYCLE STAGE

Next thesis check · unlock event:

Crypto Log

on-chain · DCA · the long-term thesis

Wallet · cold / hot: ______ Today · trade #: ______

TRADES

Date	Coin	Side	Entry	Exit	Qty	PnL

COLD STORAGE · SEED BACKED UP?

HOT WALLET · GAS FEES THIS WEEK

THESIS · WHY THIS COIN

DCA SCHEDULE · WEEKLY AMOUNT

SECURITY HYGIENE

- ☐ Seed offline
- ☐ 2FA on
- ☐ Hardware wallet
- ☐ Multi-sig
- ☐ Tested recovery
- ☐ No screenshots

MACRO · ON-CHAIN METRICS · THE CYCLE STAGE

Next thesis check · unlock event: ______

Crypto Log

on-chain · DCA · the long-term thesis

Wallet · cold / hot: ______ Today · trade #: _____

TRADES

Date	Coin	Side	Entry	Exit	Qty	PnL

COLD STORAGE · SEED BACKED UP?

HOT WALLET · GAS FEES THIS WEEK

THESIS · WHY THIS COIN

DCA SCHEDULE · WEEKLY AMOUNT

SECURITY HYGIENE

- ☐ Seed offline
- ☐ 2FA on
- ☐ Hardware wallet
- ☐ Multi-sig
- ☐ Tested recovery
- ☐ No screenshots

MACRO · ON-CHAIN METRICS · THE CYCLE STAGE

Next thesis check · unlock event: ____________

Crypto Log

on-chain · DCA · the long-term thesis

Wallet · cold / hot: ______ Today · trade #: ______

TRADES

Date	Coin	Side	Entry	Exit	Qty	PnL

COLD STORAGE · SEED BACKED UP?

HOT WALLET · GAS FEES THIS WEEK

THESIS · WHY THIS COIN

DCA SCHEDULE · WEEKLY AMOUNT

SECURITY HYGIENE

- ☐ Seed offline
- ☐ 2FA on
- ☐ Hardware wallet
- ☐ Multi-sig
- ☐ Tested recovery
- ☐ No screenshots

MACRO · ON-CHAIN METRICS · THE CYCLE STAGE

Next thesis check · unlock event: ______

Crypto Log

on-chain · DCA · the long-term thesis

Wallet · cold / hot: ______ Today · trade #: ______

TRADES

Date	Coin	Side	Entry	Exit	Qty	PnL

COLD STORAGE · SEED BACKED UP?

HOT WALLET · GAS FEES THIS WEEK

THESIS · WHY THIS COIN

DCA SCHEDULE · WEEKLY AMOUNT

SECURITY HYGIENE

- ☐ Seed offline
- ☐ 2FA on
- ☐ Hardware wallet
- ☐ Multi-sig
- ☐ Tested recovery
- ☐ No screenshots

MACRO · ON-CHAIN METRICS · THE CYCLE STAGE

Next thesis check · unlock event: ______

Crypto Log

on-chain · DCA · the long-term thesis

Wallet · cold / hot: ______ Today · trade #: ______

TRADES

Date	Coin	Side	Entry	Exit	Qty	PnL

COLD STORAGE · SEED BACKED UP?

HOT WALLET · GAS FEES THIS WEEK

THESIS · WHY THIS COIN

DCA SCHEDULE · WEEKLY AMOUNT

SECURITY HYGIENE

- ☐ Seed offline
- ☐ 2FA on
- ☐ Hardware wallet
- ☐ Multi-sig
- ☐ Tested recovery
- ☐ No screenshots

MACRO · ON-CHAIN METRICS · THE CYCLE STAGE

Next thesis check · unlock event: ______

Crypto Log

on-chain · DCA · the long-term thesis

Wallet · cold / hot: ______ Today · trade #: _____

TRADES

Date	Coin	Side	Entry	Exit	Qty	PnL

COLD STORAGE · SEED BACKED UP?

HOT WALLET · GAS FEES THIS WEEK

THESIS · WHY THIS COIN

DCA SCHEDULE · WEEKLY AMOUNT

SECURITY HYGIENE

- ☐ Seed offline
- ☐ 2FA on
- ☐ Hardware wallet
- ☐ Multi-sig
- ☐ Tested recovery
- ☐ No screenshots

MACRO · ON-CHAIN METRICS · THE CYCLE STAGE

Next thesis check · unlock event: ____________

Crypto Log

on-chain · DCA · the long-term thesis

Wallet · cold / hot: ______ Today · trade #: _____

TRADES

Date	Coin	Side	Entry	Exit	Qty	PnL

COLD STORAGE · SEED BACKED UP?

HOT WALLET · GAS FEES THIS WEEK

THESIS · WHY THIS COIN

DCA SCHEDULE · WEEKLY AMOUNT

SECURITY HYGIENE

- ☐ Seed offline
- ☐ 2FA on
- ☐ Hardware wallet
- ☐ Multi-sig
- ☐ Tested recovery
- ☐ No screenshots

MACRO · ON-CHAIN METRICS · THE CYCLE STAGE

Next thesis check · unlock event: ____________

Crypto Log

on-chain · DCA · the long-term thesis

Wallet · cold / hot: ______ Today · trade #: _____

TRADES

Date	Coin	Side	Entry	Exit	Qty	PnL

COLD STORAGE · SEED BACKED UP?

HOT WALLET · GAS FEES THIS WEEK

THESIS · WHY THIS COIN

DCA SCHEDULE · WEEKLY AMOUNT

SECURITY HYGIENE

- ☐ Seed offline
- ☐ 2FA on
- ☐ Hardware wallet
- ☐ Multi-sig
- ☐ Tested recovery
- ☐ No screenshots

MACRO · ON-CHAIN METRICS · THE CYCLE STAGE

Next thesis check · unlock event: ______

Crypto Log

on-chain · DCA · the long-term thesis

Wallet · cold / hot: ______ Today · trade #: _____

TRADES

Date	Coin	Side	Entry	Exit	Qty	PnL

COLD STORAGE · SEED BACKED UP?

HOT WALLET · GAS FEES THIS WEEK

THESIS · WHY THIS COIN

DCA SCHEDULE · WEEKLY AMOUNT

SECURITY HYGIENE

- ☐ Seed offline
- ☐ 2FA on
- ☐ Hardware wallet
- ☐ Multi-sig
- ☐ Tested recovery
- ☐ No screenshots

MACRO · ON-CHAIN METRICS · THE CYCLE STAGE

Next thesis check · unlock event: ____________

Crypto Log

on-chain · DCA · the long-term thesis

Wallet · cold / hot: ______ Today · trade #: _____

TRADES

Date	Coin	Side	Entry	Exit	Qty	PnL

COLD STORAGE · SEED BACKED UP?

HOT WALLET · GAS FEES THIS WEEK

THESIS · WHY THIS COIN

DCA SCHEDULE · WEEKLY AMOUNT

SECURITY HYGIENE

- ☐ Seed offline
- ☐ 2FA on
- ☐ Hardware wallet
- ☐ Multi-sig
- ☐ Tested recovery
- ☐ No screenshots

MACRO · ON-CHAIN METRICS · THE CYCLE STAGE

Next thesis check · unlock event: ________

Crypto Log

on-chain · DCA · the long-term thesis

Wallet · cold / hot: ______ Today · trade #: ______

TRADES

Date	Coin	Side	Entry	Exit	Qty	PnL

COLD STORAGE · SEED BACKED UP?

HOT WALLET · GAS FEES THIS WEEK

THESIS · WHY THIS COIN

DCA SCHEDULE · WEEKLY AMOUNT

SECURITY HYGIENE

- ☐ Seed offline
- ☐ 2FA on
- ☐ Hardware wallet
- ☐ Multi-sig
- ☐ Tested recovery
- ☐ No screenshots

MACRO · ON-CHAIN METRICS · THE CYCLE STAGE

Next thesis check · unlock event:

Crypto Log

on-chain · DCA · the long-term thesis

Wallet · cold / hot: ______ Today · trade #: _____

TRADES

Date	Coin	Side	Entry	Exit	Qty	PnL

COLD STORAGE · SEED BACKED UP?

HOT WALLET · GAS FEES THIS WEEK

THESIS · WHY THIS COIN

DCA SCHEDULE · WEEKLY AMOUNT

SECURITY HYGIENE

- ☐ Seed offline
- ☐ 2FA on
- ☐ Hardware wallet
- ☐ Multi-sig
- ☐ Tested recovery
- ☐ No screenshots

MACRO · ON-CHAIN METRICS · THE CYCLE STAGE

Next thesis check · unlock event:

Crypto Log

on-chain · DCA · the long-term thesis

Wallet · cold / hot: ______ Today · trade #: _____

TRADES

Date	Coin	Side	Entry	Exit	Qty	PnL

COLD STORAGE · SEED BACKED UP?

HOT WALLET · GAS FEES THIS WEEK

THESIS · WHY THIS COIN

DCA SCHEDULE · WEEKLY AMOUNT

SECURITY HYGIENE

- ☐ Seed offline
- ☐ 2FA on
- ☐ Hardware wallet
- ☐ Multi-sig
- ☐ Tested recovery
- ☐ No screenshots

MACRO · ON-CHAIN METRICS · THE CYCLE STAGE

Next thesis check · unlock event: ________________

Crypto Log

on-chain · DCA · the long-term thesis

Wallet · cold / hot: ______ Today · trade #: _____

TRADES

Date	Coin	Side	Entry	Exit	Qty	PnL

COLD STORAGE · SEED BACKED UP?

HOT WALLET · GAS FEES THIS WEEK

THESIS · WHY THIS COIN

DCA SCHEDULE · WEEKLY AMOUNT

SECURITY HYGIENE

- ☐ Seed offline
- ☐ 2FA on
- ☐ Hardware wallet
- ☐ Multi-sig
- ☐ Tested recovery
- ☐ No screenshots

MACRO · ON-CHAIN METRICS · THE CYCLE STAGE

Next thesis check · unlock event: ______

Crypto Log

on-chain · DCA · the long-term thesis

Wallet · cold / hot: ______ Today · trade #: ______

TRADES

Date	Coin	Side	Entry	Exit	Qty	PnL

COLD STORAGE · SEED BACKED UP?

HOT WALLET · GAS FEES THIS WEEK

THESIS · WHY THIS COIN

DCA SCHEDULE · WEEKLY AMOUNT

SECURITY HYGIENE

- ☐ Seed offline
- ☐ 2FA on
- ☐ Hardware wallet
- ☐ Multi-sig
- ☐ Tested recovery
- ☐ No screenshots

MACRO · ON-CHAIN METRICS · THE CYCLE STAGE

Next thesis check · unlock event:

Crypto Log

on-chain · DCA · the long-term thesis

Wallet · cold / hot: ______ Today · trade #: _____

TRADES

Date	Coin	Side	Entry	Exit	Qty	PnL

COLD STORAGE · SEED BACKED UP?

HOT WALLET · GAS FEES THIS WEEK

THESIS · WHY THIS COIN

DCA SCHEDULE · WEEKLY AMOUNT

SECURITY HYGIENE

- ☐ Seed offline
- ☐ 2FA on
- ☐ Hardware wallet
- ☐ Multi-sig
- ☐ Tested recovery
- ☐ No screenshots

MACRO · ON-CHAIN METRICS · THE CYCLE STAGE

Next thesis check · unlock event: ____________

Crypto Log

on-chain · DCA · the long-term thesis

Wallet · cold / hot: ______ Today · trade #: _____

TRADES

Date	Coin	Side	Entry	Exit	Qty	PnL

COLD STORAGE · SEED BACKED UP?

HOT WALLET · GAS FEES THIS WEEK

THESIS · WHY THIS COIN

DCA SCHEDULE · WEEKLY AMOUNT

SECURITY HYGIENE

- ☐ Seed offline
- ☐ 2FA on
- ☐ Hardware wallet
- ☐ Multi-sig
- ☐ Tested recovery
- ☐ No screenshots

MACRO · ON-CHAIN METRICS · THE CYCLE STAGE

Next thesis check · unlock event: ________________

Crypto Log

on-chain · DCA · the long-term thesis

Wallet · cold / hot: ______ Today · trade #: _____

TRADES

Date	Coin	Side	Entry	Exit	Qty	PnL

COLD STORAGE · SEED BACKED UP?

HOT WALLET · GAS FEES THIS WEEK

THESIS · WHY THIS COIN

DCA SCHEDULE · WEEKLY AMOUNT

SECURITY HYGIENE

- ☐ Seed offline
- ☐ 2FA on
- ☐ Hardware wallet
- ☐ Multi-sig
- ☐ Tested recovery
- ☐ No screenshots

MACRO · ON-CHAIN METRICS · THE CYCLE STAGE

Next thesis check · unlock event: ______

Crypto Log

on-chain · DCA · the long-term thesis

Wallet · cold / hot: ______ Today · trade #: _____

TRADES

Date	Coin	Side	Entry	Exit	Qty	PnL

COLD STORAGE · SEED BACKED UP?

HOT WALLET · GAS FEES THIS WEEK

THESIS · WHY THIS COIN

DCA SCHEDULE · WEEKLY AMOUNT

SECURITY HYGIENE

- ☐ Seed offline
- ☐ 2FA on
- ☐ Hardware wallet
- ☐ Multi-sig
- ☐ Tested recovery
- ☐ No screenshots

MACRO · ON-CHAIN METRICS · THE CYCLE STAGE

Next thesis check · unlock event: ______________________

Crypto Log

on-chain · DCA · the long-term thesis

Wallet · cold / hot: ______ Today · trade #: _____

TRADES

Date	Coin	Side	Entry	Exit	Qty	PnL

COLD STORAGE · SEED BACKED UP?

HOT WALLET · GAS FEES THIS WEEK

THESIS · WHY THIS COIN

DCA SCHEDULE · WEEKLY AMOUNT

SECURITY HYGIENE

- ☐ Seed offline
- ☐ 2FA on
- ☐ Hardware wallet
- ☐ Multi-sig
- ☐ Tested recovery
- ☐ No screenshots

MACRO · ON-CHAIN METRICS · THE CYCLE STAGE

Next thesis check · unlock event: ____________

Crypto Log

on-chain · DCA · the long-term thesis

Wallet · cold / hot: ______ Today · trade #: _____

TRADES

Date	Coin	Side	Entry	Exit	Qty	PnL

COLD STORAGE · SEED BACKED UP?

HOT WALLET · GAS FEES THIS WEEK

THESIS · WHY THIS COIN

DCA SCHEDULE · WEEKLY AMOUNT

SECURITY HYGIENE

- ☐ Seed offline
- ☐ 2FA on
- ☐ Hardware wallet
- ☐ Multi-sig
- ☐ Tested recovery
- ☐ No screenshots

MACRO · ON-CHAIN METRICS · THE CYCLE STAGE

Next thesis check · unlock event: ______

Crypto Log

on-chain · DCA · the long-term thesis

Wallet · cold / hot: ______ Today · trade #: _____

TRADES

Date	Coin	Side	Entry	Exit	Qty	PnL

COLD STORAGE · SEED BACKED UP?

HOT WALLET · GAS FEES THIS WEEK

THESIS · WHY THIS COIN

DCA SCHEDULE · WEEKLY AMOUNT

SECURITY HYGIENE

- ☐ Seed offline
- ☐ 2FA on
- ☐ Hardware wallet
- ☐ Multi-sig
- ☐ Tested recovery
- ☐ No screenshots

MACRO · ON-CHAIN METRICS · THE CYCLE STAGE

Next thesis check · unlock event: ____________

Crypto Log

on-chain · DCA · the long-term thesis

Wallet · cold / hot: ______ Today · trade #: ______

TRADES

Date	Coin	Side	Entry	Exit	Qty	PnL

COLD STORAGE · SEED BACKED UP?

HOT WALLET · GAS FEES THIS WEEK

THESIS · WHY THIS COIN

DCA SCHEDULE · WEEKLY AMOUNT

SECURITY HYGIENE

- ☐ Seed offline
- ☐ 2FA on
- ☐ Hardware wallet
- ☐ Multi-sig
- ☐ Tested recovery
- ☐ No screenshots

MACRO · ON-CHAIN METRICS · THE CYCLE STAGE

Next thesis check · unlock event: ______

Crypto Log

on-chain · DCA · the long-term thesis

Wallet · cold / hot: ______ Today · trade #: _____

TRADES

Date	Coin	Side	Entry	Exit	Qty	PnL

COLD STORAGE · SEED BACKED UP?

HOT WALLET · GAS FEES THIS WEEK

THESIS · WHY THIS COIN

DCA SCHEDULE · WEEKLY AMOUNT

SECURITY HYGIENE

- ☐ Seed offline
- ☐ 2FA on
- ☐ Hardware wallet
- ☐ Multi-sig
- ☐ Tested recovery
- ☐ No screenshots

MACRO · ON-CHAIN METRICS · THE CYCLE STAGE

Next thesis check · unlock event: ______

Crypto Log

on-chain · DCA · the long-term thesis

Wallet · cold / hot: ______ Today · trade #: ______

TRADES

Date	Coin	Side	Entry	Exit	Qty	PnL

COLD STORAGE · SEED BACKED UP?

HOT WALLET · GAS FEES THIS WEEK

THESIS · WHY THIS COIN

DCA SCHEDULE · WEEKLY AMOUNT

SECURITY HYGIENE

- ☐ Seed offline
- ☐ 2FA on
- ☐ Hardware wallet
- ☐ Multi-sig
- ☐ Tested recovery
- ☐ No screenshots

MACRO · ON-CHAIN METRICS · THE CYCLE STAGE

Next thesis check · unlock event: ______

Crypto Log

on-chain · DCA · the long-term thesis

Wallet · cold / hot: ______ Today · trade #: _____

TRADES

Date	Coin	Side	Entry	Exit	Qty	PnL

COLD STORAGE · SEED BACKED UP?

HOT WALLET · GAS FEES THIS WEEK

THESIS · WHY THIS COIN

DCA SCHEDULE · WEEKLY AMOUNT

SECURITY HYGIENE

- ☐ Seed offline
- ☐ 2FA on
- ☐ Hardware wallet
- ☐ Multi-sig
- ☐ Tested recovery
- ☐ No screenshots

MACRO · ON-CHAIN METRICS · THE CYCLE STAGE

Next thesis check · unlock event: ____________

Crypto Log

on-chain · DCA · the long-term thesis

Wallet · cold / hot: ______ Today · trade #: _____

TRADES

Date	Coin	Side	Entry	Exit	Qty	PnL

COLD STORAGE · SEED BACKED UP?

HOT WALLET · GAS FEES THIS WEEK

THESIS · WHY THIS COIN

DCA SCHEDULE · WEEKLY AMOUNT

SECURITY HYGIENE

- ☐ Seed offline
- ☐ 2FA on
- ☐ Hardware wallet
- ☐ Multi-sig
- ☐ Tested recovery
- ☐ No screenshots

MACRO · ON-CHAIN METRICS · THE CYCLE STAGE

Next thesis check · unlock event: ____________

Crypto Log

on-chain · DCA · the long-term thesis

Wallet · cold / hot: ______ Today · trade #: _____

TRADES

Date	Coin	Side	Entry	Exit	Qty	PnL

COLD STORAGE · SEED BACKED UP?

HOT WALLET · GAS FEES THIS WEEK

THESIS · WHY THIS COIN

DCA SCHEDULE · WEEKLY AMOUNT

SECURITY HYGIENE

- ☐ Seed offline
- ☐ 2FA on
- ☐ Hardware wallet
- ☐ Multi-sig
- ☐ Tested recovery
- ☐ No screenshots

MACRO · ON-CHAIN METRICS · THE CYCLE STAGE

Next thesis check · unlock event: ____________

Crypto Log

on-chain · DCA · the long-term thesis

Wallet · cold / hot: ______ Today · trade #: _____

TRADES

Date	Coin	Side	Entry	Exit	Qty	PnL

COLD STORAGE · SEED BACKED UP?

HOT WALLET · GAS FEES THIS WEEK

THESIS · WHY THIS COIN

DCA SCHEDULE · WEEKLY AMOUNT

SECURITY HYGIENE

- ☐ Seed offline
- ☐ 2FA on
- ☐ Hardware wallet
- ☐ Multi-sig
- ☐ Tested recovery
- ☐ No screenshots

MACRO · ON-CHAIN METRICS · THE CYCLE STAGE

Next thesis check · unlock event: ______

Crypto Log

on-chain · DCA · the long-term thesis

Wallet · cold / hot: ______ Today · trade #: _____

TRADES

Date	Coin	Side	Entry	Exit	Qty	PnL

COLD STORAGE · SEED BACKED UP?

HOT WALLET · GAS FEES THIS WEEK

THESIS · WHY THIS COIN

DCA SCHEDULE · WEEKLY AMOUNT

SECURITY HYGIENE

☐ Seed offline

☐ 2FA on

☐ Hardware wallet

☐ Multi-sig

☐ Tested recovery

☐ No screenshots

MACRO · ON-CHAIN METRICS · THE CYCLE STAGE

Next thesis check · unlock event: ______

Crypto Log

on-chain · DCA · the long-term thesis

Wallet · cold / hot: ______ Today · trade #: ______

TRADES

Date	Coin	Side	Entry	Exit	Qty	PnL

COLD STORAGE · SEED BACKED UP?

HOT WALLET · GAS FEES THIS WEEK

THESIS · WHY THIS COIN

DCA SCHEDULE · WEEKLY AMOUNT

SECURITY HYGIENE

- ☐ Seed offline
- ☐ 2FA on
- ☐ Hardware wallet
- ☐ Multi-sig
- ☐ Tested recovery
- ☐ No screenshots

MACRO · ON-CHAIN METRICS · THE CYCLE STAGE

Next thesis check · unlock event: ____________

Crypto Log

on-chain · DCA · the long-term thesis

Wallet · cold / hot: ______ Today · trade #: _____

TRADES

Date	Coin	Side	Entry	Exit	Qty	PnL

COLD STORAGE · SEED BACKED UP?

HOT WALLET · GAS FEES THIS WEEK

THESIS · WHY THIS COIN

DCA SCHEDULE · WEEKLY AMOUNT

SECURITY HYGIENE

- ☐ Seed offline
- ☐ 2FA on
- ☐ Hardware wallet
- ☐ Multi-sig
- ☐ Tested recovery
- ☐ No screenshots

MACRO · ON-CHAIN METRICS · THE CYCLE STAGE

Next thesis check · unlock event: ____________

Crypto Log

on-chain · DCA · the long-term thesis

Wallet · cold / hot: ______ Today · trade #: _____

TRADES

Date	Coin	Side	Entry	Exit	Qty	PnL

COLD STORAGE · SEED BACKED UP?

HOT WALLET · GAS FEES THIS WEEK

THESIS · WHY THIS COIN

DCA SCHEDULE · WEEKLY AMOUNT

SECURITY HYGIENE

- ☐ Seed offline
- ☐ 2FA on
- ☐ Hardware wallet
- ☐ Multi-sig
- ☐ Tested recovery
- ☐ No screenshots

MACRO · ON-CHAIN METRICS · THE CYCLE STAGE

Next thesis check · unlock event: ____________

I came. I bought crypto. I checked the price 47 times.

Date: ________________ **Mood:** ______________

WHAT THIS QUOTE MEANS TO ME RIGHT NOW

WHEN HAVE I LIVED THIS — OR FAILED TO?

HOW WILL I ACT ON THIS TODAY?

One word I want to carry: ____________________

Person I will share this with: __________________

Crypto: because regular investing wasn't exciting enough.

Date: ________________ **Mood:** ______________

WHAT THIS QUOTE MEANS TO ME RIGHT NOW

WHEN HAVE I LIVED THIS — OR FAILED TO?

HOW WILL I ACT ON THIS TODAY?

One word I want to carry: ____________________

Person I will share this with: ________________

My portfolio has more mood swings than I do.

Date: ________________ **Mood:** ______________

WHAT THIS QUOTE MEANS TO ME RIGHT NOW

WHEN HAVE I LIVED THIS — OR FAILED TO?

HOW WILL I ACT ON THIS TODAY?

One word I want to carry: ____________________

Person I will share this with: ________________

Buy. Hold. Check price. Repeat.

Date: ________________ Mood: _______________

WHAT THIS QUOTE MEANS TO ME RIGHT NOW

WHEN HAVE I LIVED THIS — OR FAILED TO?

HOW WILL I ACT ON THIS TODAY?

One word I want to carry: ____________________

Person I will share this with: ______________

I bought the dip. Then the dip bought another dip.

Date: ________________ Mood: _______________

WHAT THIS QUOTE MEANS TO ME RIGHT NOW

WHEN HAVE I LIVED THIS — OR FAILED TO?

HOW WILL I ACT ON THIS TODAY?

One word I want to carry: ____________________

Person I will share this with: _________________

My favorite color is crypto green.

Date: ________________ Mood: _______________

WHAT THIS QUOTE MEANS TO ME RIGHT NOW

WHEN HAVE I LIVED THIS — OR FAILED TO?

HOW WILL I ACT ON THIS TODAY?

One word I want to carry: ____________________

Person I will share this with: ____________________

I don't panic sell. I panic stare.

Date: ________________ **Mood:** ______________

WHAT THIS QUOTE MEANS TO ME RIGHT NOW

WHEN HAVE I LIVED THIS — OR FAILED TO?

HOW WILL I ACT ON THIS TODAY?

One word I want to carry: ____________________

Person I will share this with: ________________

Beginner investor today. Lambo jokes tomorrow.

Date: ________________ **Mood:** ______________

WHAT THIS QUOTE MEANS TO ME RIGHT NOW

WHEN HAVE I LIVED THIS — OR FAILED TO?

HOW WILL I ACT ON THIS TODAY?

One word I want to carry: ____________________

Person I will share this with: __________________

My crypto portfolio builds character.

Date: ________________ Mood: ______________

WHAT THIS QUOTE MEANS TO ME RIGHT NOW

WHEN HAVE I LIVED THIS — OR FAILED TO?

HOW WILL I ACT ON THIS TODAY?

One word I want to carry: ____________________

Person I will share this with: ________________

I opened my wallet and found an emotional roller coaster.

Date: ________________ **Mood:** ________________

WHAT THIS QUOTE MEANS TO ME RIGHT NOW

WHEN HAVE I LIVED THIS — OR FAILED TO?

HOW WILL I ACT ON THIS TODAY?

One word I want to carry: ______________________

Person I will share this with: ______________________

Coffee wakes me up. Crypto prices keep me awake.

Date: ________________ **Mood:** _______________

WHAT THIS QUOTE MEANS TO ME RIGHT NOW

WHEN HAVE I LIVED THIS — OR FAILED TO?

HOW WILL I ACT ON THIS TODAY?

One word I want to carry: ____________________

Person I will share this with: ________________

I've got 99 problems, and volatility is most of them.

Date: ________________ **Mood:** ______________

WHAT THIS QUOTE MEANS TO ME RIGHT NOW

WHEN HAVE I LIVED THIS — OR FAILED TO?

HOW WILL I ACT ON THIS TODAY?

One word I want to carry: ____________________

Person I will share this with: ________________

My investment strategy includes staring at charts like I understand everything.

Date: ________________ **Mood:** _______________

WHAT THIS QUOTE MEANS TO ME RIGHT NOW

WHEN HAVE I LIVED THIS — OR FAILED TO?

HOW WILL I ACT ON THIS TODAY?

One word I want to carry: ______________________

Person I will share this with: ___________________

I came for the profits. I stayed for the vocabulary.

Date: ________________ **Mood:** _______________

WHAT THIS QUOTE MEANS TO ME RIGHT NOW

WHEN HAVE I LIVED THIS — OR FAILED TO?

HOW WILL I ACT ON THIS TODAY?

One word I want to carry: ____________________

Person I will share this with: ________________

Nothing teaches patience quite like a red portfolio.

Date: ________________ **Mood:** ______________

WHAT THIS QUOTE MEANS TO ME RIGHT NOW

WHEN HAVE I LIVED THIS — OR FAILED TO?

HOW WILL I ACT ON THIS TODAY?

One word I want to carry: ____________________

Person I will share this with: ________________

My crypto wallet has trust issues.

Date: ________________ **Mood:** ________________

WHAT THIS QUOTE MEANS TO ME RIGHT NOW

WHEN HAVE I LIVED THIS — OR FAILED TO?

HOW WILL I ACT ON THIS TODAY?

One word I want to carry: ______________________

Person I will share this with: ______________________

I don't need a roller coaster. I own crypto.

Date: ________________ **Mood:** _______________

WHAT THIS QUOTE MEANS TO ME RIGHT NOW

WHEN HAVE I LIVED THIS — OR FAILED TO?

HOW WILL I ACT ON THIS TODAY?

One word I want to carry: _____________________

Person I will share this with: ___________________

Today's lesson: apparently it can dip again.

Date: ________________ **Mood:** ______________

WHAT THIS QUOTE MEANS TO ME RIGHT NOW

WHEN HAVE I LIVED THIS — OR FAILED TO?

HOW WILL I ACT ON THIS TODAY?

One word I want to carry: ____________________

Person I will share this with: ________________

My portfolio and I are currently taking some space.

Date: ________________ **Mood:** ________________

WHAT THIS QUOTE MEANS TO ME RIGHT NOW

WHEN HAVE I LIVED THIS — OR FAILED TO?

HOW WILL I ACT ON THIS TODAY?

One word I want to carry: ____________________

Person I will share this with: ____________________

Crypto taught me that 'long term' can feel very long.

Date: ________________ **Mood:** ______________

WHAT THIS QUOTE MEANS TO ME RIGHT NOW

WHEN HAVE I LIVED THIS — OR FAILED TO?

HOW WILL I ACT ON THIS TODAY?

One word I want to carry: ____________________

Person I will share this with: ________________

I bought because the chart looked friendly.

Date: ________________ **Mood:** ______________

WHAT THIS QUOTE MEANS TO ME RIGHT NOW

WHEN HAVE I LIVED THIS — OR FAILED TO?

HOW WILL I ACT ON THIS TODAY?

One word I want to carry: ____________________

Person I will share this with: ________________

My financial education now includes mysterious three-letter abbreviations.

Date: ________________ **Mood:** _______________

WHAT THIS QUOTE MEANS TO ME RIGHT NOW

WHEN HAVE I LIVED THIS — OR FAILED TO?

HOW WILL I ACT ON THIS TODAY?

One word I want to carry: ____________________

Person I will share this with: ________________

One minute I'm an investor. The next I'm Googling what I just bought.

Date: ________________ **Mood:** ______________

WHAT THIS QUOTE MEANS TO ME RIGHT NOW

WHEN HAVE I LIVED THIS — OR FAILED TO?

HOW WILL I ACT ON THIS TODAY?

One word I want to carry: ____________________

Person I will share this with: __________________

Keep calm and stop refreshing the price.

Date: ________________ **Mood:** _______________

WHAT THIS QUOTE MEANS TO ME RIGHT NOW

WHEN HAVE I LIVED THIS — OR FAILED TO?

HOW WILL I ACT ON THIS TODAY?

One word I want to carry: ____________________

Person I will share this with: ________________

My portfolio is diversified across several different ways to make me nervous.

Date: ________________ **Mood:** _______________

WHAT THIS QUOTE MEANS TO ME RIGHT NOW

WHEN HAVE I LIVED THIS — OR FAILED TO?

HOW WILL I ACT ON THIS TODAY?

One word I want to carry: ____________________

Person I will share this with: ____________________

I finally understand blockchain... until someone asks me to explain it.

Date: ________________ **Mood:** ______________

WHAT THIS QUOTE MEANS TO ME RIGHT NOW

WHEN HAVE I LIVED THIS — OR FAILED TO?

HOW WILL I ACT ON THIS TODAY?

One word I want to carry: ______________________

Person I will share this with: ________________

My crypto journey is powered by curiosity and questionable amounts of coffee.

Date: ________________ **Mood:** ________________

WHAT THIS QUOTE MEANS TO ME RIGHT NOW

WHEN HAVE I LIVED THIS — OR FAILED TO?

HOW WILL I ACT ON THIS TODAY?

One word I want to carry: ____________________

Person I will share this with: ____________________

Every beginner has a moment called, 'Wait... where did my crypto go?'

Date: ________________ **Mood:** ______________

WHAT THIS QUOTE MEANS TO ME RIGHT NOW

WHEN HAVE I LIVED THIS — OR FAILED TO?

HOW WILL I ACT ON THIS TODAY?

One word I want to carry: ____________________

Person I will share this with: ________________

The market never sleeps, which seems unnecessarily dramatic.

Date: ________________ **Mood:** ______________

WHAT THIS QUOTE MEANS TO ME RIGHT NOW

WHEN HAVE I LIVED THIS — OR FAILED TO?

HOW WILL I ACT ON THIS TODAY?

One word I want to carry: ____________________

Person I will share this with: __________________

May your passwords be safe and your candles be green.

Date: ________________ **Mood:** ______________

WHAT THIS QUOTE MEANS TO ME RIGHT NOW

WHEN HAVE I LIVED THIS — OR FAILED TO?

HOW WILL I ACT ON THIS TODAY?

One word I want to carry: ____________________

Person I will share this with: ________________

www.ingramcontent.com/pod-product-compliance
Lightning Source LLC
LaVergne TN
LVHW010732061126
851857LV00014B/1453